Keto
BREAD

Keto
BREAD

A Guide for the Absolute Beginner

MARIANN ANDERSSON | PHOTOGRAPHY BY MARTIN SKREDSVIK

Skyhorse Publishing

Contents

Loaves, Baguettes, Buns, and Rolls

Crispbreads and Crackers

Bread-Based Meals

Introduction

WHEN I STARTED FOLLOWING THE LOW-CARB lifestyle a few years ago, my biggest challenge by far was giving up bread. Up until then, bread and grain-based foods had been the foundation of my daily diet—looking back, I realize I was probably addicted to the stuff. While I didn't miss pasta at all, doing away with sandwiches or slices of crispbread layered with butter and cheese was another thing altogether.

At first I thought I could get away with simply eating thinner pieces of crispbread. However, when I began to understand the havoc that gluten was wreaking on my health, I decided to give up gluten-laden foods entirely, including those beloved slices of crispbread I still occasionally treated myself to.

Many of us deal with stress on a daily basis. There doesn't seem to be enough hours in the day to get everything done, including cooking a nutritious and satisfying breakfast, when so much else competes for our attention. That's why in many ways the humble sandwich is a perfect solution—and because it can be eaten on the run. What about brown-bagging lunch? Again, a sandwich is a great option for eating at the office—but then again, who has the time to fix it before rushing out the door in the morning? This may be a slight exaggeration, but it's still uncomfortably close to reality for many of us with busy schedules.

This is where my nutritious yet low-carb bread recipes come into play. In Sweden we call a loaf of bread "matbröd," which can be translated into English as "food bread." The name is fitting; in this book the sandwich is elevated to its rightful status as proper food, because all of my breads can be considered food in their own right , as opposed to mere vessels for more wholesome meals. They are nutritional powerhouses. Who could ask for more?

I've stretched my imagination and experimented with herbs and spices in order to include as many different styles and varieties of bread as possible in this book. You'll find many recipes for loaves and rolls, both white and dark, as well as crispbreads, pizza, empanadas, and lots more!

Wishing you all a life filled with joy and good health,

Mariann

Mariann

Low-Carb High-Fat Breads

Bread baked according to Low-Carb High-Fat guidelines differs from traditionally baked bread in that it contains very few carbohydrates and is often combined with an elevated amount of fat.

Further significant differences from grain-based bread are the absence of gluten and the inclusion of a large amount of eggs. Eggs contain high levels of nutritiously beneficial protein, vitamins, minerals, and micronutrients; when incorporated into dough, they help to turn out bread that is both filling and deeply satisfying. We don't call eggs a superfood for nothing.

Even LCHF bread doesn't usually contain enough fat by itself, so we help it conform closer to the LCHF formula by spreading our sandwiches with delicious grass-fed butter and by adding slices of aged cheese, ham, sliced deli sausage, or other delicious fatty fillings. By doing so, we get an LCHF sandwich that is food through and through. Furthermore, since LCHF bread is naturally gluten-free, it's perfect for those who are gluten-intolerant, and its low-carb content makes it highly suitable for diabetics.

Breads Made with Grains

In early civilizations, our ancestors didn't turn to grains for nutrition. People have inhabited the planet for millions of years, but have only been cultivating grains in Scandinavia for approximately four thousand years. This has been too short a time for our digestive tract to become adjusted to the daily ingestion of grains from our modern diet.

Starch
All grains such as oats, wheat, rye, and corn contain glucose in the form of starch, which elevates blood sugar. Those of us who eat a low-carbohydrate diet should aim to keep our intake of starch as low as possible.

Gluten
Our commonly used grains—wheat, rye, and corn—also contain gluten. Gluten is a vegetable protein that can irritate the lining of the small intestine and bring on gluten intolerance and celiac disease.

Celiac disease, also known as celiac sprue, is an autoimmune disease that develops when the small intestine becomes hyper-sensitive to gluten. The intestinal villi (small fingerlike projections in the lining of the intestinal wall) deteriorate, which disrupts the uptake of nutrients from ingested food, and may cause large amounts of the protein in that food to leak into the body.

Celiac disease is often linked to other autoimmune disorders, such as type 1 diabetes and rheumatism. Many affected by celiac disease are unaware of their condition because they do not feel sick or suffer from stomachaches. If left untreated, however, celiac disease can lead to fatigue, anemia, infertility, and weight loss; it can also cause a variety of stomach ailments.

Gluten intolerance manifests itself in such a wide array of symptoms that it can be challenging to pinpoint gluten as the source of trouble. It often brings on diarrhea, constipation, and gas, and can be painful. It can also exacerbate the severity of other allergies as well as chronic conditions such as asthma. Gluten can damage the intestine to the point where the enzyme that breaks down lactose is lost. More and more people are diagnosed as lactose intolerant, which in some cases could be traced back to their gluten-damaged intestine reacting to lactose.

These days, many grocery stores carry bread labeled "Low Carb" or "LCHF." It is important to note, however, that much of this commercially manufactured bread contains gluten as a main ingredient. Worse, it might even include wheat flour. These breads may be low in carbohydrates, but are they healthy? Not in my world—my world is gluten-free.

Baking Healthy Breads

From a practical standpoint there is a huge advantage to baking low-carb bread: it's quick! There's no need to set aside time for the rising of the dough—you simply whisk the batter together, let it rest for a few minutes, and a short while later the dough is ready to form and bake. If the dough doesn't seem firm enough to the touch, add additional fiber husk or coconut flour. Start by adding half a tablespoon of fiber husk or one tablespoon of coconut flour to the batter, let the dough rest a minute, then check the consistency. Be sure to add only a little fiber at a time, because if you add too much the bread might end up too dry and crumbly.

Be aware that some types of dough start out sticky on purpose so that the bread doesn't become too dense. Wet your palms with cold water to make the dough easier to handle. If the finished product still doesn't seem airy enough, try decreasing the amount of flour when mixing the dough.

If you want to bake the loaves in loaf pans, line a six-cup loaf pan with parchment paper and pour in the batter. Freestanding loaves baked on baking sheets will need more flour in the dough to make them easier to form and able to retain their shape while baking.

I usually place the items on the middle shelf and use the convection function on my oven. However, this book uses temperatures for conventional ovens, so if you have a convection oven, simply decrease the given temperature by fifteen degrees Celsius. For Fahrenheit, reduce the temperature by twenty-five degrees and keep the time consistent.

Baking times do vary by oven, so if you're unsure of the heat generated by your oven, make the first batch of bread a test; take note if you need to make adjustments in temperature or baking times in the future.

For a crisper crust on the bread, spray or brush the dough with some water immediately before putting the bread in the oven, and repeat this process a few times while baking. I find it easiest to use a spray bottle and cold water.

Please keep in mind that Low-Carb High-Fat bread does not keep as long as a conventional loaf of bread, so if you want to store bread longer than twenty-four hours, keep it in a plastic bag in the refrigerator. Later, when you are ready to enjoy a slice, reheat the bread quickly in the microwave for a softer consistency. If you prefer to store the bread at room temperature, avoid plastic bags and wrap the bread in a towel or baking cloth instead. Crispbreads will keep longer than other bread, but it is imperative to store them in an airtight container to keep them dry—a cookie tin is ideal. All breads from the recipes in this book keep exceptionally well in the freezer. If you want pre-sliced bread ready for the toaster, cut the loaf into sections and lay the slices on a baking sheet. Freeze them on the baking sheet for one hour. Remove the frozen bread slices from the baking sheet, insert them in a plastic bag and seal tightly, then put the bag back in the freezer.

Toast, microwave, or heat the slices in the oven. For the sake of convenience, bake the recipes in double batches.

My recipes use eggs, cream, crème fraîche, cream cheese, Greek yogurt, quark, sour cream; Parmesan, feta, and various types of grated cheese; salted butter and olive oil. Coconut, almond, and a variety of nut flours are also combined with different kinds of seeds. If using salted seeds, decrease the amount of salt in the recipe. Spices and herbs are used for seasoning.

Liquid ingredients such as butter, cream, crème fraîche, quark, Greek yogurt, and cream cheese are interchangeable as long as you follow the given amounts. Sour cream can be used to impart the tangy taste of sourdough. If you prefer moister bread, add some grated cheese to the batter.

If you need to make your recipes dairy-free, substitute the called-for dairy ingredient with water, using the same amount of liquid as written in the recipe. Different sorts of fats can be switched as well: if the recipe calls for butter, you can use a good quality coconut oil instead. In some cases, olive oil can be used, but use it with caution, as olive oil has a relatively low smoking point compared to butter and coconut oil and breaks down at high temperatures.

The recipes are high in protein due to their large amount of egg, which gives them a nice golden sheen. The amount of protein in each recipe makes it unnecessary to add any whey protein powder, but should you still wish to add some, approximately 1.6 ounces should do the trick. Keep in mind that the extra whey powder will increase the carbohydrate count of the finished baked goods.

I use baking powder instead of yeast in my recipes. Yeast is activated by sugar, so I avoid it because I don't really know how much of the sugar remains after baking. However, if you have sensitive taste buds and can detect a certain rough quality to the bread baked with baking powder, try reducing or even removing the baking powder entirely from the recipe. Of course, the trade-off will be bread with a far denser consistency due to the lack of a raising agent.

Pantry Staples

Baking Low-Carb High-Fat requires specific pantry staples to replace conventional baking flours. Below you'll find a list of what I use instead of wheat flour, and at the back of the book I have provided useful links to merchants selling these products.

Almond Flour

You don't need to blanch the almonds and remove their skins if you grind or mix your own flour. Ready-ground flours are available; you may be able to find reduced-fat almond flour. If you want to use the latter kind, you'll need to reduce the flour amount in the recipes or you'll end up with dry and crumbly bread.

Carbohydrate content varies between 4 and 12 grams per 3½ ounces (100 grams), depending on the brand and origin of the almonds.

Coconut Flour

There are several products on the market with varying carbohydrate content. Make sure you get coconut flour and not ground coconut flakes, which will give your bread a pronounced coconut flavor and the wrong texture. Its carbohydrate content varies between 2 and 4 carbohydrates per ounce (28 grams) depending on the brand.

Psyllium husk (whole and ground, unflavored)

Unflavored psyllium husks are sold both whole and as a ground powder. Powdered psyllium makes for dense bread. Psyllium seed husk helps to produce a bread-like texture, as it replaces gluten to a certain extent. The husk is highly absorbent, so although the bread will not have the same airy texture as gluten-rich bread, its inclusion produces a moister loaf. There is no carbohydrate content since the husk is pure fiber.

Oat Fiber

Oat fiber is a lightweight white powdered fiber. It is a pure fiber, not flour, and is used as filler. Carbohydrate and calorie content is zero per ounce (28 grams).

 tips!

If oat fiber is unavailable, you can substitute whole psyllium husk or coconut flour. See individual recipe for specific amounts to use.

NutraFiber Flakes

These fiber flakes are made from sugar beets. They look a little like oat flakes and are used to add more of a rustic, chewy feel to the bread. The flakes have good absorbency, and a little goes a long way. The carbohydrate content is 25 grams per 3½ ounces (100 grams).

Nuts and Seeds

Sunflower, pumpkin, flax and sesame seeds and hazelnuts (filberts), and walnuts can all be used whole, crushed, coarsely chopped, or finely ground. Try mixing several types for variety. Carbohydrate content will vary depending on the nuts and seeds used, but a small amount only ups the carb content slightly.

 tips!

If using salted seeds, decrease amount of salt in recipe.

A Note About Eggs

Swedish "large" eggs weigh approximately 2½ ounces (71 grams), so I suggest using US extra-large eggs.

What is Quark?

Quark is a traditional eastern European fermented dairy product. If quark is unavailable, substitute with two parts full-fat ricotta cheese to one part crème fraîche.

Wishing you all Happy Baking!

Loaves, Baguettes, Buns, and Rolls

Brunch Rolls

These are favorites at Sunday brunch, but can also be the perfect accompaniment to an elegant dinner. Poppy seeds add delicious crunch to each bite, but can be omitted from the recipe to no ill effect if they are unavailable to you.

6 rolls

Ingredients:
1 oz (30 g) butter
3 extra-large or 4 large eggs
½ cup (100 ml) whipping cream
½ cup (100 ml) full-fat cheese
  (aged if possible), grated
1 cup (200 ml) almond flour
3 tbsps coconut flour
3 tbsps whole psyllium husks
¼ cup (50 ml) oat fiber*
½–1 tbsp whole psyllium husk
  or 2–3 tbsps coconut flour
½ tsp salt
2 tsps baking powder
Poppy seeds for garnish

 tips!

For a crisper crust, fill a small spray bottle with cold water and mist the rolls just before baking. Repeat once or twice during baking.

*Oat fiber can be replaced with ½–1 tbsp whole psyllium husk or 2–3 tbsps coconut flour.

Directions:
Preheat the oven to 375°F (190°C) and line a baking sheet with parchment paper. Melt the butter.

In a medium bowl, beat the eggs with a handheld electric mixer until light and airy, approximately three minutes. Add melted and cooled butter and whipping cream and mix thoroughly. Fold in the cheese.

In a separate bowl, mix dry ingredients, then blend thoroughly into the batter. Let mixture rest at least ten minutes.

Shape six evenly formed rolls and place them on the parchment-covered baking sheet.

Sprinkle the rolls with poppy seeds. Bake in the middle of oven until golden, about twenty minutes.

Cool, uncovered, on a wire rack.

Cheese Rolls

The world's best cheese rolls! I absolutely love their crispy crust and the delicious taste of melted cheese!

6–8 rolls

Ingredients:
1 oz (30 g) butter
3 extra-large or 4 large eggs
½ cup (100 ml) crème fraîche
¾ cup (150 ml) full-fat cheese (aged if possible), grated
1 cup (200 ml) almond flour
3 tbsps coconut flour
4 tbsps whole psyllium husks
½ cup (100 ml) sesame seeds
½ tsp salt
2 tsps baking powder

 tips!

For a crisper crust, fill a small spray bottle with cold water and mist the rolls just before baking. Repeat once or twice during baking.

Directions:
Preheat the oven to 375°F (190°C). Melt the butter. Line a baking sheet with parchment paper.

In a medium bowl, beat eggs with a handheld electric mixer until light and airy, approximately three minutes. Add melted and cooled butter and crème fraîche and mix thoroughly. Fold in half a cup of grated cheese.

In a separate bowl, mix the rest of ingredients, then blend thoroughly into the batter. Let mixture rest at least ten minutes.

Shape six to eight rolls and place them on the parchment-lined baking sheet. Sprinkle the rest of the grated cheese over the rolls. Bake in middle of oven until cheese is melted and the color is golden, approximately twenty to twenty-five minutes.

Cool, uncovered, on a wire rack.

Rustic Rolls

These wonderfully tasty rolls make a perfect side to a steaming bowl of comforting soup. Don't omit the Parmesan, as it gives these rolls a special touch!

6 rolls

Ingredients:
1 oz (30 g) butter
3 extra-large or 4 large eggs
½ cup (100 ml) quark*
½ cup (100 ml) almond flour
3 tbsps coconut flour
¼ cup (50 ml) flax seed
¼ cup (50 ml) oat fiber**
3 tbsps NutraFiber Flakes, ground
½ tsp salt
2 tsps baking powder
½ cup (100 ml) Parmesan cheese, finely
   grated (as covering for rolls)

Directions:
Preheat oven to 375°F (190°C). Melt the butter. Line a baking sheet with parchment paper.

In a medium bowl, whisk eggs with a handheld electric mixer until light and airy, approximately three minutes. Add melted and cooled butter and Quark.

In a separate bowl, mix dry ingredients well, then blend thoroughly into the batter. Let the mixture rest at least ten minutes.

Shape six rolls, roll them in the finely grated Parmesan cheese, and place them on the parchment-covered baking sheet.

Bake the rolls in the middle of the oven until golden, approximately twenty minutes.

Cool, uncovered, on a wire rack.

 tips!

For a crisper crust, fill a small spray bottle with cold water and mist the rolls just before baking. Repeat once or twice during baking.

*If quark is unavailable, substitute with two parts full-fat ricotta to one part crème fraîche.
**Oat fiber can be replaced with ½–1 tbsp whole psyllium husk or 2–3 tbsps coconut flour.

Cumin-Scented Rolls

These rolls are reminiscent of Danish cumin rolls. If cumin is a new taste for you, I hope this recipe will become one of your favorites!

4–6 rolls

Ingredients:
3 extra-large or 4 large eggs
3½ oz (100 g) cream cheese, softened
1 cup (200 ml) almond flour
3 tbsps whole psyllium husks
2 tbsps coconut flour
2 tbsps NutraFiber Flakes, ground
2 tbsps flaxseeds
1½ tsps whole cumin seed
2 tsp baking powder
½ tsp salt
Whole cumin seed for garnish

Directions:
Preheat oven to 375°F (190°C). Line a baking sheet with parchment paper.

In a medium bowl, beat eggs with a handheld electric mixer until light and airy, for approximately three minutes.

Add the softened cream cheese and blend into a smooth batter.

In a separate bowl, mix dry ingredients, then blend thoroughly into the batter. Let mixture rest approximately ten minutes.

Shape four to six rolls and place them on the parchment-lined baking sheet. Sprinkle the rolls with whole cumin seeds and bake in middle of the oven until the color is golden brown, about twenty minutes.

Cool under a cloth on a wire rack.

Nutty Buns—Sourdough Taste-A-Likes

Delicious rolls to enjoy as a snack with your favorite drink or with a much-loved meal. The yogurt's tang blends wonderfully with the robust flavor of the walnuts.

6 rolls

Ingredients:
4 extra-large or 5 large eggs
¾ cup (150 ml) full-fat Greek yogurt
½ cup (100 ml) almond flour
1 cup (200 ml) walnuts, finely ground
  or mixed plus some extra for garnish
¼ cup (50 ml) NutraFiber Flakes, as flakes
1½ tbsps whole psyllium husks
1 tsp baking powder
½ tsp salt

 tips!

To increase sourdough taste, use a mixture of yogurt and sour cream. Remember that this adds some extra carbohydrates.

Directions:
Preheat oven to 375°F (190°C). Line a baking sheet with parchment paper.

In a medium bowl, beat eggs with a handheld electric mixer until light and airy, for approximately three minutes. Add the yogurt and blend well.

In a separate bowl, mix the rest of the ingredients, then blend thoroughly into the egg batter. Let mixture rest at least ten minutes.

With the help of a wet spoon, form six slightly flattened buns on the parchment-lined baking sheet. Scatter ground walnuts on the buns and bake in the middle of the oven until they are golden brown, about twenty-five minutes.

Cool under a cloth on a wire rack.

Yogurt and Seed Buns

A flax and sunflower seed version of Nutty Buns, fully of chewy goodness!

6 rolls

Ingredients:
4 extra-large or 5 large eggs
¾ cup (150 ml) Greek yogurt
1 cup (200 ml) almond flour
½ cup (100 ml) flaxseeds
½ cup (100 ml) sunflower seeds, chopped
2 tbsps coconut flour
2 tbsps whole psyllium husks
1 tsp baking powder
½ tsp salt
Whole sunflower seeds for garnish

Directions:
Preheat oven to 375°F (190°C). Line a baking sheet with parchment paper.

In a medium bowl, beat eggs with a handheld electric mixer until light and airy, approximately three minutes. Add yogurt and blend to a smooth batter.

In a separate bowl, mix dry ingredients, then blend thoroughly into the batter. Let mixture rest at least ten minutes.

With the help of a wet spoon, shape six square, slightly flattened buns on the parchment-lined baking sheet. Sprinkle the buns with whole sunflower seeds. Bake in the middle of the oven until golden brown, approximately twenty-five minutes.

Cool under a cloth on a wire rack.

 tips!

For more intense flavor, add ground bread spices. If using salted sunflower seeds, decrease amount of salt in recipe.

Swedish Tea Buns

Make it a special occasion with these buns slathered in fresh butter to go with a selection of aged cheeses and a mix of fresh salad greens. Serve with a glass of milk or a big cup of your favorite tea.

6 tea buns

Ingredients:
3½ oz (100 g) butter
5 extra-large or 6 large eggs
¾ cup (150 ml) almond flour
½ cup (100 ml) coconut flour
1 tsp baking powder
½ tsp salt

Directions:
Preheat oven to 375°F (190°C).
Melt butter. Line a baking sheet with parchment paper.

In a medium bowl, beat eggs with a handheld electric mixer until light and airy, approximately three minutes. Add melted and cooled butter and blend well.

In a separate bowl, mix dry ingredients, then blend thoroughly into the batter. Let mixture rest at least ten minutes.

Space six mounds well apart on the parchment-lined baking sheet. With wet fingers or the back of a wet spoon, flatten the mounds into round buns approximately half an inch high. Bake in the middle of the oven until golden brown, about twenty minutes.

Cool under a cloth on a wire rack.

Rustic Tea Buns

A rustic version of the Swedish Tea Buns, these pair exceptionally well with thickly sliced ham. Top with a slice of vine-ripened tomato and some minced parsley.

6 rustic buns

Ingredients:
5 extra-large or 6 large eggs
¾ cup (150 ml) whipping cream
¼ cup (50 ml) coconut flour
½ cup (100 ml) almond flour
¼ cup (50 ml) NutraFiber Flakes
¼ cup (50 ml) NutraFiber Flakes, ground
¼ cup (50 ml) oat fiber*
1 tbsp whole psyllium husks
½ tbsp ground bread spices (fennel,
  cumin, and anise seeds—or buy ready
  ground)
½ tsp salt
2 tsps baking powder

Directions:
Preheat oven to 375°F (190°C). Line a baking sheet with parchment paper.

In a medium bowl, beat eggs with a handheld electric mixer until light and airy, approximately three minutes. Add whipping cream and blend well.

In a separate bowl, mix dry ingredients, then blend thoroughly into the batter. Let mixture rest at least ten ten minutes.

Space six mounds well apart on the parchment-lined baking sheet. With wet fingers or the back of a wet spoon, flatten the mounds into round buns, approximately half an inch high.

Bake in the middle of the oven until golden brown, about twenty minutes. Cool under a cloth on a wire rack.

*Oat fiber can be replaced with ½–1 tbsp whole psyllium husk or 2–3 tbsps coconut flour.

Zucchini Baguettes

Load these attractive loaves up with smoked ham slices or other smoked meats. The grated zucchini is the secret behind their great texture!

2 big or 4 small baguettes

Ingredients:
4 extra-large or 5 large eggs
¾ cup (150 ml) zucchini, finely grated
¾ cup (150 ml) almond flour
2 tbsps whole psyllium husks
½ cup (100 ml) sesame seeds
½ tsp salt
1½ tsp baking powder

Optional: chopped walnuts, cinnamon

 tips!

For that extra touch, add a quarter (¼) cup coarsely chopped walnuts and 1 tsp of ground cinnamon to the mixture.

Directions:
Preheat oven to 375°F (190°C). Line a baking sheet with parchment paper.

In a medium bowl, beat eggs with a handheld electric mixer until light and airy, approximately three minutes. Add grated zucchini and fold in thoroughly.

In a separate bowl, mix the dry ingredients, then blend thoroughly into the batter. Let the mixture rest at least ten minutes.

Using wet hands, shape two big or four small baguettes and place on the parchment-lined baking sheet. With a sharp knife, make three decorative cuts across the baguettes.

Bake in the middle of the oven until golden brown, about thirty minutes for the larger size and about twenty to twenty-five minutes for the smaller size.

Cool under a cloth on wire rack.

Baguette with Mediterranean Flavors

These seductive, hearty baguettes brim with feta cheese and Mediterranean herbs.

2 big or 4 small baguettes

Ingredients:
4 extra-large or 5 large eggs
3½ oz (100 g) feta cheese, mashed
  with fork
¾ cup almond flour
2 tbsps whole psyllium husks
2 tbsps coconut flour
2 tbsps dried Mediterranean
  oregano (do not use Mexican)
1 tbsp dried thyme
1½ tsp baking powder

Directions:
Preheat oven to 375°F (190°C). Line a baking sheet with parchment paper.

In a medium bowl, beat eggs with a handheld electric mixer until light and airy, approximately three minutes. Fold mashed feta cheese into the batter.

In a separate bowl, mix dry ingredients, then blend thoroughly into the batter. Let mixture rest at least ten minutes.

Using wet hands, shape two big or four smaller baguettes and place on the parchment-lined baking sheet.

Bake in the middle of the oven until golden brown, about thirty minutes for the large size and about twenty to twenty-five minutes for the smaller size.

Cool under a cloth on a wire rack.

Focaccia with Red Onion and Parmesan

Make room on the buffet table for this impressive loaf of bread. Parmesan and rosemary sprigs give this focaccia its distinctive taste.

Serves 6–8

Ingredients:
¼ cup (50 ml) red onion, minced finely
1 oz (30 g) butter
4 extra-large or 5 large eggs
7 oz (200 g) cream cheese, softened
½ cup (100 ml) Parmesan cheese, grated
1 cup (200 ml) almond flour
2 tbsps coconut flour
1 tbsp whole psyllium husks
1 tsp salt
2 tsps baking powder
Fresh rosemary leaves
Kosher salt

Directions:
Preheat oven to 375°F (190°C). Fry onion in butter and set aside. Line a 6" x 10" (15 cm x 25 cm) baking pan with parchment paper or butter and dust it with coconut flour.

In a large bowl, beat eggs with a handheld electric mixer until light and airy, approximately three minutes. Add the softened cream cheese and mix until batter is smooth. Fold in fried onion with its butter and the grated Parmesan.

In a separate bowl, mix dry ingredients, then blend thoroughly into the batter. Let mixture rest at least ten minutes.

Spread the mixture evenly in the baking pan and scatter with rosemary leaves and some Kosher salt.

Bake the focaccia in the middle of the oven until it is golden brown, about thirty minutes. Remove from pan and cool under a cloth on a wire rack.

 tips!

Flavor variations:
• 2 tbsps dried rosemary, 1 tsp garlic powder, and a drizzle of olive oil.
• 3 tbsps dried Mediterranean oregano and ½ cup (100 ml) chopped Kalamata olives.
• 4 to 5 chopped sun-dried tomatoes and chopped fresh basil.
• Replace 3½ oz (100 g) of cream cheese with ½ cup (100 ml) crushed tomatoes. Sprinkle with basil.

Poppy Seed-Crusted Monkey Bread

Luxurious party fare with a marvelous aroma of Parmesan! This bread goes perfectly with consommé or a delectable stew and makes a great addition to any buffet table.

Makes 11 pieces

Ingredients:

8 extra-large or 10 large eggs
½ cup (100 ml) water
¼ cup (50 ml) olive oil
1 cup (200 ml) Parmesan cheese, grated
4½ tbsps (75 ml) coconut flour
1¼ cup (250 ml) almond flour
½ cup (100 ml) sesame seeds
3 tbsps whole psyllium husks
2 tsps baking powder
Lightly whipped egg for glazing
Poppy seeds
Extra butter and coconut flour to dust
    baking pan

Directions:

Preheat oven to 375°F (190°C). Line the bottom of a springform pan—8¼" (21 cm) in diameter—with parchment paper. Butter and dust the edges with coconut flour.

In a large bowl, beat eggs with a handheld electric mixer until light and airy, approximately three minutes. Add water and oil and mix thoroughly. Fold in Parmesan.

In a separate bowl, mix dry ingredients, then blend thoroughly into the batter. Let mixture rest at least ten minutes.

Separate the dough into eleven pieces and shape each into a round ball. Place the balls side by side in the pan, brush with egg wash, and sprinkle liberally with poppy seeds.

Bake in the middle of the oven until golden brown, about thirty to forty minutes. Remove from pan and cool under a cloth on a wire rack.

Walnut Rings

These are incredibly delicious! A side of aged cheese and some cucumber or pepper slices will only enhance their good looks.

1 large or 4 small rings

Ingredients:
1½ oz (30 g) butter
5 extra-large or 6 large eggs
½ cup (100 ml) Greek yogurt
½ cup (100 ml) full-fat cheese
   (preferably aged), grated
½ tbsp whole cumin seeds
1 cup (200 ml) walnuts, finely ground
½ cup (100 mll) almond flour
4½ tbsps coconut flour
1¼ tbsps whole psyllium husks
2 tsps baking powder
Whole cumin seeds for garnish

Directions:
Preheat oven to 375°F (190°C).
Melt butter. Line a baking sheet with parchment paper.

In a medium bowl, beat eggs with a handheld electric mixer until light and airy, approximately three minutes. Add melted and cooled butter, yogurt, and grated cheese. Mix well.

Crush the cumin seeds with mortar and pestle (or use a Magic Bullet-type blender) and add to the rest of dry ingredients in a separate bowl.
Add dry ingredients to the batter and mix well. Let the mixture rest at least ten minutes.

Using wet hands, shape dough either into four smaller rings or one large ring. Sprinkle rings with whole cumin seeds.

Bake in the middle of the oven, twenty minutes for the smaller rings or about thirty minutes for the large ring. Cool under a cloth on a wire rack.

Toasted Loaf

The aroma of fresh toast in the morning is a great way to start the day, so indulge yourself! Add slices of egg, some shrimp, a dollop of mayonnaise, and for that final Swedish touch, top with a few sprigs of fresh dill.

1 loaf

Ingredients:
1¾ oz (50 g) butter
10 extra-large or 12 large eggs
½ tsp salt
¾ cup (150 ml) coconut flour
2 tbsps whole psyllium husks
1–2 tsps baking powder
Sesame seeds for garnish

 tips!

This bread is excellent if toasted on the highest level or even twice.

Directions:
Preheat oven to 375°F (190°C). Melt butter. Line a 6-cup (1419-ml) loaf pan with parchment paper.

In a large bowl, beat eggs with a handheld electric mixer until light and airy, approximately three minutes. Add melted and cooled butter together with the salt. Mix well.

In a separate bowl, mix dry ingredients, then blend thoroughly into the batter. Let mixture rest at least ten minutes.

Spread the mixture evenly in the loaf tin and sprinkle sesame seeds over the surface. Bake in middle of oven until golden brown, about fifty minutes.

Remove loaf from pan and cool under a cloth on a wire rack.

Sandwich Loaf

Whether the menu lists a decadent oven-baked sandwich, something quick from the grill, or even just plain toast, this is the all-purpose loaf for the job.

1 sandwich loaf

Ingredients:
1¾ oz (50 g) butter
8 extra-large or 10 large eggs
½ cup (100 ml) full-fat cheese (preferably aged), grated
¼ cup (50 ml) coconut flour
1 cup (200 ml) almond flour
½ cup (100 ml) sesame seeds
3 tbsps whole psyllium seeds
½ tsp salt
2 tsp baking powder
Poppy seeds for garnish

Directions:
Preheat oven to 375°F (190°C). Melt butter. Line a 6-cup (1419-ml) loaf pan with parchment paper.

In a large bowl, beat eggs with a handheld electric mixer until light and airy, approximately three minutes. Add melted and cooled butter, fold in the grated cheese, and mix thoroughly.

In a separate bowl, mix dry ingredients, then blend thoroughly into the batter. Let mixture rest at least ten minutes.

Spread mixture evenly in prepared loaf pan and sprinkle poppy seeds on the surface. Bake in the middle of the oven until the loaf is golden brown, about fifty minutes. Remove loaf from pan and cool under a cloth on a wire rack.

Rustic Pumpkinseed Loaf

Slathered with chicken liver pâté, studded with pickles, or topped with delicate fresh cucumber slices, a thick slice of this bread makes for a satisfying meal.

1 loaf

Ingredients:
1¾ oz (50 g) butter
¼ cup (50 ml) NutraFiber Flakes
8 extra-large or 10 large eggs
½ cup (100 ml) quark*
¼ cup (50 ml) coconut flour
½ cup (100 ml) almond flour
½ cup (100 ml) flax seeds
¼ cup (50 ml) oat fiber**
½ cup pumpkin seeds
2 tsps baking powder
½ tsp salt
Pumpkins seeds for garnish

*If quark is not available, substitute with 2 parts full-fat ricotta to 1 part crème fraîche.
**Oat fiber can be replaced with ½–1 tbsp whole psyllium husk or 2–3 tbsps coconut flour. If using salted pumpkin seeds, decrease salt in recipe.

Directions:
Preheat oven to 375°F (190°C). Melt butter, add NutraFiber Flakes, and mix well. Line baking sheet with parchment paper.

In a large bowl, beat eggs with a handheld electric mixer until light and airy, approximately three minutes. Add cooled NutraFiber Flakes and butter mixture and quark, blending well.

In a separate bowl, mix dry ingredients and blend them thoroughly into the egg/NutraFiber Flake mixture. Let mixture rest about ten to fifteen minutes.

Shape the dough into a loaf, sprinkle pumpkin seeds on the surface, and put the loaf on the prepared baking sheet. Bake in the middle of the oven until the loaf is a nice golden brown, about fifty minutes. Cool under a cloth on a wire rack.

Rustic Lingonberry Loaf

We Swedes love our lingonberries, which grow wild in the countryside, and no smorgasbord is complete without a jar of lingonberry jam or jelly. Here we have added lingonberries to a rustic loaf of bread, which nicely complement the spices in the bread. Cranberries make an excellent substitute if you can't find lingonberries.

1 loaf

Ingredients:
1¾ oz (50 g) butter
8 extra-large or 10 large eggs
½ cup (100 ml) quark*
½ cup (100 ml) fresh or frozen lingonberries
3 tbsps coconut flour
½ cup (100 ml) almond flour
½ cup (100 ml) hazelnuts (filberts), ground or chopped finely
½ cup (100 ml) flax seeds
½ cup (100 ml) NutraFiber Flakes
¼ cup (50 ml) oat fiber**
1½ tbsps bread spices (anise, fennel, and cumin seeds), ground or store-bought
2 tsps baking powder
½ tsp salt
Whole cumin seeds for garnish

*If quark is not available, substitute with two parts full-fat ricotta to one part crème fraîche.
**Oat fiber can be replaced with ½–1 tbsp whole psyllium husk or 2–3 tbsps coconut flour.

Directions:
Preheat oven to 375°F (190°C). Melt butter. Line a 6-cup (1419-ml) loaf pan with parchment paper. If using frozen berries, do not defrost.

In a large bowl, beat eggs with a handheld electric mixer until light and airy, approximately three minutes. Add melted and cooled butter and the quark. Fold in lingonberries or cranberries.

In a separate bowl, mix dry ingredients, then blend thoroughly into the batter.

Spread mixture in prepared loaf pan and sprinkle with whole cumin seeds. Bake in middle of oven until bread is golden brown, about fifty minutes. Remove pan and cool under a cloth on a wire rack.

Sunflower Seed Loaf

Slices of this loaf slathered in fresh butter and topped with aged cheese alongside a good cup of strong coffee? Highly recommended any time!

1 loaf

Ingredients:
1¾ oz (50 g) butter
8 extra-large or 10 large eggs
½ cup (100 ml) Greek yogurt
¾ cup (150 ml) almond flour
½ cup NutraFiber Flakes
½ cup (100 ml) sunflower seeds
½ cup (100 ml) oat fiber*
3 tbsps whole psyllium husks
2 tsps baking powder
½ tsp salt
Sunflower seeds for garnish

Directions:
Preheat oven to 375°F (190°C).
Melt butter. Line a baking sheet with parchment paper.

In a large bowl, beat eggs with a handheld electric mixer until light and airy, approximately three minutes. Add the melted and cooled butter and the yogurt and blend well.

In a separate bowl, mix dry ingredients, then incorporate thoroughly into the batter. Let the mixture rest about ten to fifteen minutes.

Shape a loaf and place on the prepared baking sheet. Sprinkle the loaf with sunflower seeds. Bake in middle of oven until the loaf is a golden brown, about fifty minutes. Cool under a cloth on a wire rack.

*Oat fiber can be replaced with ½–1 tbsp whole psyllium husk or 2–3 tbsps coconut flour.

If using salted seeds, decrease amount of salt in recipe.

Walnut Square Loaf

Walnuts are veritable health nuggets, bursting with nutrition and flavor. Here, the coarsely chopped nuts add a delicate crispness and full-bodied taste to the bread.

1 square loaf

Ingredients:
1¾ oz (50 g) butter
8 extra-large or 10 large eggs
3½ oz (100 g) cream cheese, softened
¼ cup (50 ml) coconut flour
1 cup (200 ml) almond flour
¾ cup (150 ml) walnuts, finely ground or
   mixed, plus 3 tbsps for sprinkling
3 tbsps whole psyllium husks
¼ cup (50 ml) oat fiber*
2 tsps baking powder
½ tsp salt
¼ cup (50 ml) walnuts, coarsely chopped

Directions:
Preheat oven to 375°F (190°C).
Melt butter. Line a baking sheet with parchment paper.

In a large bowl, beat eggs with a handheld electric mixer until light and airy, approximately three minutes. Add melted and cooled butter and cream cheese and mix to a smooth batter.

In a separate bowl, mix dry ingredients, then blend thoroughly into the batter. Let mixture rest at least ten to fifteen minutes.

Shape a 6" x 6" (15 cm x 15 cm) plump loaf and place it on the prepared baking sheet. With a sharp knife, make a few slashes in the surface and sprinkle with the three tbsps of finely ground walnut flour.

Bake in middle of oven until loaf is golden brown, about fifty minutes. Cool under a cloth on a wire rack.

 tips!

For a more sourdough-like effect, use half the amount of butter and add ¼ cup (50 ml) cup of sour cream.

*Oat fiber can be replaced with ½–1 tbsp whole psyllium husk or 2–3 tbsps coconut flour.

Olive and Feta Loaf

With a Greek salad, tzatziki, and a small glass of Retsina alongside this loaf, your table has just moved a little closer to the Mediterranean!

1 loaf

Ingredients:
8 extra-large or 10 large eggs
¼ cup (50 ml) good quality olive oil (preferably extra virgin)
3½ oz (100 g) feta cheese, mashed with fork
¼ cup–½ cup (50 ml–100 ml) Kalamata olives, coarsely chopped
2 tbsps dried rosemary
4½ tbsps (75 ml) coconut flour
1¼ cups (250 ml) almond flour
¼ cup (50 ml) oat fiber*
3 tbsps whole psyllium husks
2 tsps baking powder
Dried rosemary for sprinkling

*Oat fiber can be replaced with ½–1 tbsp whole psyllium husk or 2–3 tbsps coconut flour.

Directions:
Preheat oven to 375°F (190°C). Mash feta cheese with fork. Line baking sheet with parchment paper.

In a large bowl, beat eggs with a handheld electric mixer until light and airy, approximately three minutes. Add oil and blend well. Fold in feta, olives, and rosemary.

In a separate bowl, mix dry ingredients, then blend thoroughly into the batter. Let mixture rest at least ten to fifteen minutes.

Shape a loaf and place it on the prepared baking sheet. Sprinkle with dried rosemary. Bake in the middle of the oven until loaf is golden brown, about fifty minutes. Cool under a cloth on a wire rack.

 tips!

Bake the bread in a small brownie pan. Then break it into pieces and use as perfect scoops for tzatziki. Try another kind of taste by adding some finely chopped sundried tomatoes to the batter.

Basil-Scented Loaf

An ideal accompaniment to a rustic soup or stew. I prefer to use dried basil in this recipe, but feel free to try fresh basil and see which result you like best.

1 loaf

Ingredients:
1 oz (30 g) butter
8 extra-large or 10 large eggs
3½ oz (100 g) feta cheese, mashed
½ cup (100 ml) coconut flour
1¼ cup (250 ml) almond flour
½ cup (100 ml) oat fiber*
2 tbsps whole psyllium husks
2–4 tbsps fresh basil or 1–2 tbsp
  dried basil
Small amount of whipping cream for
  glazing

Directions:
Preheat oven to 375°F (190°C). Melt butter. Mash feta with a fork. Line baking sheet with parchment paper.

In a large bowl, beat eggs with a handheld electric mixer until light and airy, approximately three minutes. Fold in feta and the melted and cooled butter.

In a separate bowl, mix dry ingredients, then blend thoroughly into the batter. Let mixture rest at least ten to fifteen minutes.

Shape a loaf, place it on the prepared baking sheet, and brush the loaf with whipping cream. Bake in the middle of the oven until the loaf is golden brown, about fifty minutes. Cool under a cloth on a wire rack.

*Oat fiber can be replaced with ½ to 1 tbsp whole psyllium husk or 2–3 tbsps coconut flour.

Spicy French Loaf

Loaded with fresh spices, the name suits this bread to a T. Fresh butter complements its full-bodied flavor in a simple snack; for a bit of added sophistication, try it with an interesting cheese platter.

1 loaf

Ingredients:
1 cup (200 ml) whipping cream
1 tbsp bread spices (fennel, anise, cumin), ground or store-bought
1 tsp ginger, ground
1 tsp cinnamon, ground
5 extra-large or 6 large eggs
½ cup (100 ml) pumpkin seeds, chopped
½ cup (100 ml) walnuts, finely chopped
¾ cup (150 ml) almond flour
¼ cup (50 ml) coconut flour
2 tbsps whole psyllium husks
1 tsp kosher salt
2 tsps baking soda
Butter and sliced almonds for baking pan

 tips!

If using salted seeds, decrease salt in recipe.

Directions:
Preheat oven to 375°F (190°C). Put whipping cream and spices in a small saucepan and bring quickly to a boil. Let cool. Butter a bundt pan, preferably silicon or nonstick, and cover with sliced almonds.

In a large bowl, beat eggs with a handheld electric mixer until light and airy, approximately three minutes. Add the cooled spice-cream.

In a separate bowl, mix dry ingredients, then blend thoroughly into the batter. Let batter rest ten minutes.

Spread the batter carefully in the prepared pan and bake in the middle of the oven for about thirty to forty minutes.

Let the bread rest a few minutes in the pan, then cool under a cloth or the pan on a wire rack.

Skillet Bread

Need something easy to pack for a road trip? From this recipe that's faster than fast food, you'll get a satisfying bread to use as the base for an al fresco lunch.

1 loaf

Ingredients:
3 extra-large or 4 large eggs
¼ cup plus 1 tbsp (75 ml) Greek yogurt
1½ tbsps whole psyllium husks
¾ cup (150 ml) almond flour
1 tsp baking powder
1 tbsp bread spice (fennel, anise, cumin),
  ground or store-bought
½ tsp salt
Butter or coconut oil for frying
Pumpkin seeds for garnish (optional)

 tips!

For more texture, add some sesame or flax seeds to the batter. Need something more filling with a stronger flavor? Add ½ cup (100 ml) grated aged cheese to the batter.

Directions:
In a medium bowl, beat the eggs with a handheld electric mixer until light and airy, approximately three minutes. Add yogurt and blend well.

In a separate bowl, mix dry ingredients, then blend thoroughly into the batter. Let the mixture rest at least ten minutes.

Heat frying pan on medium heat and add a small amount of butter or coconut oil. Turn heat to medium and pour mixture in frying pan. With the aid of a spatula, carefully shape the mixture into a round form. If you wish, sprinkle surface with sunflower seeds.

On medium heat, fry first side about seven minutes until golden brown, then continue on the other side for approximately the same amount of time. Keep a close watch so as not to burn the bread.

Cool under a cloth on a wire rack.

Simple Loaf

This is the perfect bread for a picnic! Afraid it might get squashed during transport? Simply bake it in an aluminum pan, and when the bread has cooled, add the lid to the pan and you're ready to hit the road!

6–8 pieces or 12 slices

Ingredients:
1¾ oz (50 g) butter, plus extra for pan
½ cup (100 ml) whipping cream
6 extra-large or 8 large eggs
1 cup (200 ml) oat fiber*
½ cup (100 ml) sesame seeds
2 tbsps coconut flour
1 tbsp whole psyllium husks
½ tsp bread spice (fennel, anise, cumin), ground or store-bought
1 tsp baking powder

 tips!

For even pieces, score bread with a sharp knife before baking. To feed larger appetites, add ½ cup (100 ml) grated aged cheese to the batter.

*Oat fiber can be replaced with ½–1 tbsp whole psyllium husk or 2–3 tbsps coconut flour.

Directions:
Preheat oven to 375°F (190°C). Melt butter, cool, and add cream. Butter a 6" x 10" (15 cm x 25 cm) loaf pan and dust with coconut flour.

In a medium bowl, beat eggs with a handheld electric mixer until light and airy, approximately three minutes. Add butter-cream mixture, blending well.

In a separate bowl, mix dry ingredients, then blend thoroughly into the batter. Let mixture rest at least ten minutes.

Spread mixture evenly in pan and bake in the middle of the oven until bread is golden brown, about twenty-five to thirty minutes.

Remove pan and cool under a cloth on a wire rack.

Rustic Loaf

Do you prefer chewier, hardier bread from the pan? This rustic loaf is more substantial, but just as delicious as its simple loaf cousin.

6–8 pieces or 14 slices

Ingredients:
1¾ oz (50 g) butter, plus some for the
  pan
½ cup (100 ml) whipping cream
6 extra-large or 8 large eggs
1 cup (200 ml) Oat fiber*, plus extra for
  the pan
½ cup (100 ml) NutraFiber Flakes, ground
½ cup (100 ml) flax seeds
2 tbsp coconut flour
1 tsp bread spices (anise, fennel, cumin),
  ground or store-bought
1 tsp baking powder
1 tsp salt

 tips!

For even pieces, score bread with a sharp knife before baking.
To feed larger appetites, add ½ cup (100 ml) grated aged cheese to the batter.

*Oat fiber can be replaced with ½–1 tbsp whole psyllium husk or 2–3 tbsps coconut flour.

Directions:
Preheat oven to 375°F (190°C).
Melt butter, cool, and add cream. Butter a 6″ x 10″ (15 cm x 25 cm) loaf pan and dust with coconut flour.

In a medium bowl, beat eggs with a handheld electric mixer until light and airy, approximately three minutes. Add butter-cream mixture and blend well.

In a separate bowl, mix dry ingredients, then blend thoroughly into the batter. Let mixture rest at least ten minutes.

Spread the mixture evenly in prepared pan and bake in the middle of the oven until golden brown, about twenty-five to thirty minutes.

Let cool under a cloth on a wire rack.

Swedish Christmas Loaf

There can be no Swedish Christmas without spice-filled breads! Try a slice of this loaf topped with special Swedish Christmas ham and add some mustard for the full effect!

1 loaf

Ingredients:
1¾ oz (50 g) butter
1 tsp ginger, ground
1 tsp candied bitter (Seville) orange rind or bitter orange extract
1 tsp allspice, ground
8 extra-large or 10 large eggs
½ cup (100 ml) whipping cream, low-carb and gluten-free
½ cup (100 ml) coconut flour
1 cup (200 ml) almond flour
¼ cup (50 ml) oat fiber*
¼ cup (50 ml) NutraFiber Flakes, ground
2 tsp baking powder

 tips!

Water is a good substitute if you would prefer not to use cream.

*Oat fiber can be replaced with ½–1 tbsp whole psyllium husk or 2–3 tbsps coconut flour.

Directions:
Preheat oven to 375°F (190°C). Melt butter and add spices. Line a 6-cup (1419-ml) loaf pan with parchment paper.

In a large bowl, beat eggs with a handheld electric mixer until light and airy, approximately three minutes. Add butter-spice mixture and beer and blend well.

In a separate bowl, mix dry ingredients, then blend thoroughly into the batter. Let mixture rest at least ten minutes.

Spread mixture evenly in loaf pan and bake in the middle of the oven until golden brown, about fifty minutes.

Let cool under a cloth on a wire rack.

Crispbreads and Crackers

Cinnamon-Scented Crispbread

A basic recipe that delights with each new spice concoction. Don't fancy cinnamon? Try a variety of other spice combinations to discover your new personal favorites to add to your recipe box.

12 small crispbreads

Ingredients:
1 extra-large egg
½ cup (100 ml) water
½ tsp salt
½ cup (100 ml) sunflower seeds, coarsely chopped or mixed
¼ cup (50 ml) flax seeds
¼ cup (50 ml) coconut flour
¼ cup (50 ml) almond flour
1 tsp baking powder
2 tsps cinnamon, ground

Directions:
Preheat oven to 350°F (175°C). In a bowl, whisk together egg, water, and salt.

In a separate bowl, mix dry ingredients, then blend thoroughly into the batter. Let mixture rest at least five minutes.

Place dough between two pieces of oiled parchment paper. With a rolling pin, flatten and roll the dough into a thin rectangle, approximately 8" x 10" (20 cm x 25 cm).

Remove upper paper layer and, with a sharp knife, cut the rectangle into twelve pieces.

Place rectangles, still on parchment, on a baking sheet and bake in the middle of the oven for about thirty minutes.

Turn off the heat and leave crispbread in the oven for another thirty to forty minutes.

Cool slightly on baking sheet, then switch to an uncovered wire rack to cool completely.

 tips!

Try different spice variations, such as 1 tsp ground cardamom or 1 tbsp dried rosemary or basil with some kosher salt on top. Whole or crushed cumin seeds—about 1 tbsp—also tastes great. Or why not ½–1 tsp each of crushed anise and fennel? Another interesting combination is 1 tsp cinnamon mixed with 1 tsp of ground ginger.
If using salted seeds, decrease amount of salt in recipe.

Sesame Seed Crackers

Sesame seeds, in addition to being delicious, are a rich source of minerals and vitamin E. Added to these crackers, they provide a nutty, full-bodied flavor.

6–8 crackers

Ingredients:
1 extra-large egg
½ cup (100 ml) water
1 tsp salt
½ cup (100 ml) sesame seeds
¼ cup (50 ml) flax seeds
¼ cup (50 ml) coconut flour
1½ tbsps (25 ml) NutraFiber Flakes
1 tsp baking powder

 tips!

Feel free to change the shape of any of the crispbreads or crackers.

Directions:
Preheat the oven to 350°F (175°C). Line a baking sheet with parchment paper.

In a bowl, whisk together egg, water, and salt. In a separate bowl, mix dry ingredients, then blend thoroughly into the batter. Let mixture rest at least five minutes.

Drop 6 to 8 mounds onto the prepared baking sheet and carefully flatten into 4" to 4½" (10 cm–12 cm) round crackers with your fingertips. Neaten the edges as much as possible.

Bake in the middle of the oven for about thirty minutes. Turn off the heat and leave the crackers in the oven for another thirty to forty minutes.

Cool slightly on baking sheet, then switch to an uncovered wire rack to cool completely.

Multi-Seed Crispbread

A versatile crispbread that's terrific for all sorts of occasions: party time, an everyday meal, or a great all-purpose snack.

12 small crispbreads

Ingredients:
1 extra-large egg
½ cup (100 ml) water
½ tsp salt
½ cup (100 ml) flax seeds
½ cup (100 ml) sesame seeds
½ cup (100 ml) pumpkin seeds, coarsely chopped
¼ cup (50 ml) coconut flour
1 tsp baking powder
Pumpkin seeds and kosher salt for garnish

 tips!

If using salted seeds, decrease amount of salt in recipe.

Directions:
Preheat oven to 350°F (175°C). In a bowl, whisk together egg, water, and salt.

In a separate bowl, mix dry ingredients, then blend thoroughly into the batter. Let mixture rest at least five minutes.

Place dough between two pieces of oiled parchment paper. With a rolling pin, flatten and roll the dough into a thin rectangle, approximately 8" x 10" (20 cm x 25 cm). Remove upper paper layer and, with a sharp knife, cut the rectangle into twelve pieces. Sprinkle with pumpkin seeds and some kosher salt.

Place rectangles, still on parchment, on a baking sheet and bake in the middle of the oven for about forty-five minutes.

Turn off the heat and leave crispbread in the oven for another thirty to forty minutes.

Cool slightly on baking sheet, then switch to an uncovered a wire rack to cool completely.

Swedish Christmas Crackers

Cloves, ginger, and candied bitter orange peel or orange extract give these crackers their characteristic Swedish flavor. To be true to the season, slather them with fresh butter and add some good-sized slices of Edam cheese or special Christmas ham—and don't forget to add a dollop of mustard!

8 crackers

Ingredients:
1 extra-large egg
½ cup (100 ml) water
½ tsp salt
1 tsp ginger, ground
½ tsp candied bitter (Seville) orange peel,
   ground or bitter orange extract
½ tsp cloves, ground
½ cup (100 ml) sesame seeds
¼ cup (50 ml) flax seeds
¼ cup (50 ml) coconut flour
¼ cup (50 ml) NutraFiber Flakes, ground
1 tsp baking powder

 tips!

Feel free to change the shape of any of the crispbreads or crackers.

Directions:
Preheat the oven to 350°F (175°C). Line a baking sheet with parchment paper.

In a bowl, whisk together egg, water, and salt. In a separate bowl, mix dry ingredients, then blend thoroughly into the batter. Let mixture rest at least five minutes.

Drop eight mounds onto the prepared baking sheet and carefully flatten into 4" to 4½" (10 cm–12 cm) round crackers with your fingertips. Neaten the edges as much as possible.

Bake in the middle of the oven for about forty-five minutes. Turn off the heat and leave the crackers in the oven for another thirty to forty minutes.

Cool slightly on baking sheet, then switch to an uncovered wire rack to cool completely.

Bread-Based Meals

Full-Flavored Hot Dog Buns

This is not your plain traditional fare—my hot dog buns are full of flavor, thanks to their French mustard and thyme.

8 buns

Ingredients:
1¾ oz (50 g) butter
6 extra-large or 8 large eggs
¾ cup (150 ml) water
½ cup (100 ml) coconut flour
1 cup (200 ml) almond flour
2 tbsps whole psyllium husks
2 tsps baking powder
1 tsp dried thyme
2 tsps French mustard

Directions:
Preheat oven to 375°F (190°C).
Melt butter and allow it to cool. Line a baking sheet with parchment paper.

In a large bowl, beat eggs with a handheld electric mixer until light and airy, approximately three minutes. Add butter, mustard, and water. Blend well.

In a separate bowl, mix dry ingredients, then blend thoroughly into the batter. Let mixture rest at least ten to twenty minutes.

With wet palms, shape eight 4-inch (10-cm) buns. Place on baking sheet and bake in the middle of the oven for about twenty-five minutes. Let cool under a cloth on a wire rack.

 tips!

If your hot dogs are spicy, you might prefer traditional hot dog buns—just leave out the French mustard and thyme.

Hamburger Buns

This says "summer" to me: a hamburger fresh off the grill on a freshly baked bun!

6 large or 8 small buns

Ingredients:
1¾ oz (50 g) butter
6 extra-large or 8 large eggs
¾ cup (150 ml) water
1 cup (200 ml) almond flour
½ cup (100 ml) coconut flour
½ cup (100 ml) sesame seeds
1 tbsp whole psyllium seeds
1 tsp baking powder
½ tsp salt
Sesame seeds for garnish

 tips!

For more full-bodied flavor but less coconut flour, replace ¼ cup (50 ml) of the coconut flour with 1 tbsp whole psyllium husks and ½ cup (100 ml) grated aged cheese.

Directions:
Preheat oven to 375°F (190°C). Melt butter and allow it to cool. Line baking sheet with parchment paper.

In a large bowl, beat eggs with a handheld electric mixer until light and airy, approximately three minutes. Add butter and water. Blend well.

In a separate bowl, mix dry ingredients, then blend thoroughly into the batter. Let mixture rest at least ten to twenty minutes.

Widely space six mounds on the prepared baking sheet. Use wet palms or the back of a wet spoon to form round buns about half an inch (1 cm) high. Sprinkle with sesame seeds.

Bake the middle of the oven for about twenty to twenty-five minutes until buns have a golden color.

Let cool under a cloth on a wire rack.

Tortillas

Tortillas are as easy to make as they are easy to eat, and are delicious to boot. These handy wraps can be fried or—if you prefer—baked in a convection oven.

4 large tortillas

Ingredients:
4 extra-large or 5 large eggs
3½ oz cream cheese, softened
2 tbsps whole psyllium husks
2 tbsps coconut flour
½ tsp salt

Filling as desired (for examples, see Tips below)

Directions:
If using a convection oven, preheat to 350°F (175°C). Oil two sheets of parchment paper.

In a medium bowl, beat eggs with a handheld electric mixer until light and airy, approximately three minutes. Add the cream cheese and blend until smooth.

In a separate bowl, mix dry ingredients, then blend thoroughly into the batter. Let mixture rest at least fifteen minutes.

Separate mixture into four equal pieces. Place one at a time between two pieces of oiled parchment paper, and shape a tortilla with a rolling pin.

Melt some butter or coconut oil in a frying pan over low heat. Remove upper parchment and turn the tortilla into the frying pan before removing the second piece of parchment. Fry on low heat until the tortilla is golden brown. Turn the tortilla and fry the other side.

If using a convection oven, place tortillas on a baking sheet and bake for about ten minutes.

Let cool under a cloth on a wire rack.

 tips!

Add tuna fish salad to your tortilla: Whip ¾ cup (150 ml) crème fraîche until stiff, add ¼ cup (50 ml) full-fat mayonnaise and 1 well-drained can of tuna. Season with salt and freshly ground pepper. Sprinkle with finely chopped leek and grated cucumber. Add a crisp lettuce leaf if desired.

Pizza

This practical crust can be prebaked and frozen for later use. When you're ready to assemble your pizza, defrost the crust slightly, cover with your favorite sauce and toppings, and finish baking.

1 crust

Ingredients:
2 extra-large or 3 large eggs
4 tbsp water
½ cup (100 ml) coconut flour
2 tsps whole psyllium husk
1 tsp baking powder
½ tbsp dried, crumbled Mediterranean oregano
½ tsp salt

Toppings as desired

 tips!

I make my sauce from tomato purée, virgin olive oil, onion powder, and dried basil.

Add ¼ cup (50 ml) of grated aged cheese to the batter, and you have an out-of-this-world delicious pizza crust! To make a larger version, just double the ingredients.

Directions:
Preheat oven to 420°F (215°C). Oil two sheets of parchment paper.

In a bowl, beat eggs with a handheld electric mixer until light and airy, approximately three minutes. Add water.

In a separate bowl, mix dry ingredients, then blend thoroughly into the batter. Let mixture rest at least ten minutes.

Place mixture between two pieces of oiled parchment paper and use a rolling pin to roll out pizza crust, barely a quarter-inch (½-cm) thick.

Prebake crust for about ten minutes. Lower heat to 375°F (190°C).

Cover pizza crust with tomato sauce or purée and add desired toppings—tuna, mussels, ham, yellow onion, pepper slices, or whatever else you like. Top with a generous layer of grated full-fat cheese and return the pizza to the oven for another ten minutes. Sprinkle with dried oregano and serve.

Delectable Pizza Buns

These are a favorite of mine, and since they're perfect for road trips, I always make sure to include a few in my picnic basket. Fill them with whatever takes your fancy!

8 buns

Ingredients:
1¾ oz (50 g) butter
6 extra-large or 8 large eggs
½ cup (100 ml) whipping cream
¼ cup (50 ml) coconut flour
½ cup (100 ml) almond flour
4 tbsps whole psyllium husks
½ tsp salt
1 tsp baking powder

Filling:
¼ cup plus 1 tbsp (65 ml) tomato purée
3 tbsps good quality olive oil
Generous 1 cup (200 ml) ham, cooked,
  cut into thin strips (julienned)
Generous 1 cup (200 ml) full-fat cheese,
  grated, plus some for sprinkling
2 tbsps dried Mediterranean oregano,
  crumbled, plus some for sprinkling

Directions:
Preheat oven to 375°F (190°C). Melt butter and allow it to cool. Mix tomato purée and olive oil. Julienne ham. Grate cheese. Oil two sheets of parchment paper.

In a bowl, beat eggs with a handheld electric mixer until light and airy, approximately three minutes. Add butter and cream, blending well.

In a separate bowl, mix dry ingredients, then blend thoroughly into batter. Let mixture swell at least ten minutes.

Put mixture between the prepared parchment sheets and, with a rolling pin, make a 10″ x 12″ (25 cm x 30 cm) rectangle. Carefully remove upper sheet of parchment.

Spread the rectangle with tomato puree and oil mixture. First, cover with ham, then cheese, and sprinkle with oregano. Roll rectangle into a thick roll. Cut roll into eight even slices and place the slices in large paper muffin cups. Sprinkle with extra cheese and oregano.

Bake in the middle of the oven for about twenty-five minutes. Cool under a cloth on a wire rack.

 tips!

A simple and practical variation: Add grated cheese, chopped sun-dried tomatoes, julienned ham, olive oil, and dried oregano directly to the bun mixture. Spoon mixture into eight large paper muffin cups and bake as above.

Empanadas

A superb start to a festive dinner!

4 empanadas

Ingredients:

1¾ oz (50 g) butter

4 extra-large or 5 large eggs

3½ oz (100 g) cream cheese, softened

½ cup (100 ml) coconut flour

½ cup (100 ml) almond flour

2 tbsps whole psyllium husks

½ tsp salt

1 tsp baking powder

Filling:

7 oz (200 g) smoked salmon, julienned
   into fine strips

2 large eggs, hard-boiled, chopped

3 tbsps dill, finely chopped

3 tbsps chives, finely chopped

½–¾ cup (100 ml–150 ml) full-fat
   cheese, grated

1 egg, lightly beaten, for glazing

Directions:

Preheat oven to 375°F (190°C). Melt butter and allow it to cool. Julienne salmon and chop dill and chives. Grate cheese. Mix filling. Line baking sheet with parchment paper. Oil two sheets of parchment paper.

In a large bowl, beat eggs with a handheld electric mixer until light and airy, approximately three minutes. Add butter and cream cheese. Blend until batter is smooth.

In a separate bowl, mix dry ingredients, then blend thoroughly into batter. Let mixture rest at least fifteen minutes.

Separate dough into four pieces. Place the dough, one piece at a time, between prepared parchment sheets and make four round circles with a rolling pin. Remove upper parchment sheet and add filling to middle of circles. By lifting the lower parchment sheet, carefully fold the circle of dough in half and press down. Pinch together edges to stop filling from leaking out.

Lift the parchment with the empanada still attached, cover empanada with one hand, and turn it over. Release paper and place empanada on the prepared baking sheet. Repeat with next three circles.

Brush dough with egg wash and bake in the middle of the oven for twenty minutes. Cool on a wire rack.

 tips!

Other scrumptious filling ideas: Spicy meat mixture with grated cheese; grated cheese and julienned ham mixed with various herbs; crispy bacon and julienned leeks with cream cheese or cottage cheese.

Mediterranean Muffins

Great for potlucks and picnics! Easy to make, easy to carry, and best of all, easy to eat!

6 muffins

Ingredients:
1¾ oz (50 g) butter
4 extra-large or 5 large eggs
½ cup (100 ml) whipping cream
½ tsp salt
½ cup (100 ml) full-fat cheese, grated
¼ cup (50 ml) coconut flour
¼ cup (50 ml) oat fiber*
1 tbsp whole psyllium husks
1 tsp baking powder
Freshly ground black pepper

Filling:
6–8 olives, chopped
2 sun-dried tomatoes, chopped
¼ red onion, finely minced
1¾ oz (50 g) feta cheese, coarsely
  chopped
1–2 tbsps good quality olive oil

 tips!

Play with different variations—your
imagination is your limit!

*Oat fiber can be replaced with
½–1 tbsp whole psyllium husk or
2–3 tbsps coconut flour.

Directions:
Preheat oven to 375°F (190°C).
Melt butter and allow it to cool. Prepare
filling.

In a bowl, beat eggs with handheld
electric mixer until light and airy,
approximately three minutes. Add butter
and cream and blend until smooth. Add
salt and pepper and fold in cheese.

In a separate bowl, mix dry ingredients,
then blend thoroughly into batter. Let
mixture rest at least five minutes.

Fill paper or silicon muffin tins with
mixture halfway, add a dollop of filling,
and cover with more of the mixture.

Bake in the middle of the oven for about
fifteen minutes. Cool under a cloth on a
wire rack.

Greek Quiche

A balmy summer's night in the company of friends, a scrumptious quiche, and a glass of chilled wine...

4 large servings

Ingredients:
3½ oz (100 g) butter, at room temperature
¼ cup (50 ml) oat fiber*
¾ cup (150 ml) almond flour
1½ tbsps whole psyllium husks
½ tsp salt
3 large or 2 extra-large eggs
Salt and freshly ground black pepper

Filling:
3 large or 2 extra-large eggs
1 cup (200 ml) crème fraîche or
  whipping cream
5¼ oz (150 g) feta cheese, coarsely
  chopped
5¼ oz (150 g) fresh spinach, chopped
½ tsp salt

Directions:
Preheat oven to 420°F (215°C).

With a pastry cutter, mix butter, oat fiber, almond flour, whole psyllium husks, and salt. Mix in eggs and make a smooth pastry dough. Press pastry into a 9" (20 cm) pie form. Chill in fridge for at least thirty minutes.

Filling: Beat eggs vigorously. Blend in crème fraîche or whipping cream, salt, and freshly ground pepper. Add spinach last.

Prebake quiche pastry for about five minutes. Fill pastry shell with filling and bake for an additional twenty minutes.

 tips!

For a more rustic pastry shell, add a ¼ cup (50 ml) NutraFiber Flakes. If you like sesame seeds add ¼ cup (50 ml) sesame seeds to pastry mixture. Don't want feta or spinach? Substitute with other flavorful cheeses and vegetables.

*Oat fiber can be replaced with ½–1 tbsp whole psyllium husk or 2–3 tbsps coconut flour.

Swedish Sandwich Torta Deluxe with variations

A true Swedish classic! An irresistible abundance and variety of fillings and trimmings, equally delicious made into a sandwich log or cut into triangles, tapas-style. (Can be made one day in advance. Keep refrigerated and wrapped in plastic wrap. Garnish one hour before serving).

Serves 8–10

Ingredients:
1½ oz (40 g) butter
12 extra-large or 15 large eggs
½ cup (100 ml) coconut flour
½ cup (100 ml) almond flour
3 tbsps whole psyllium husks
1 tsp salt
3 tsps baking powder
Coconut flour for dusting pans

Skagen Filling:
2¼ lb (1 kg) shrimp in shell or
  1 lb (450 g) peeled, cooked, and in brine
  or 1½–2 cups (300–400 ml) frozen
½ cup (100 ml) full-fat mayonnaise
½ cup (100 ml) crème fraîche or 1 cup
  (200 ml) Greek yogurt (at least 2% fat)

OR
mix half of each
2 tbsps dill, chopped
2 tsps fresh lemon juice
2 tbsps red onion, finely minced
Salt and freshly ground black pepper
1 jar red or yellow roe (optional)

Salad Filling:
½ head crisp lettuce, julienned in fine
  strips
1 cup (200 ml) crème fraîche
½ cup (100 ml) full-fat mayonnaise

Smoked Salmon Filling:
1 lb (450 g) smoked salmon, thinly sliced
4 extra-large or 5 large hard-boiled eggs
1 bunch watercress
1 cup (200 ml) crème fraîche
1 tbsp fresh lemon juice
Salt and freshly ground black pepper

Garnish:
½ cup (100 ml) full-fat mayonnaise
½ cup (100 ml) crème fraîche
Lemon juice, optional
½ lb (225 g) smoked salmon, thinly sliced
1 lb (450 g) shrimp cooked and peeled
2 oz (50 g) tin red or yellow roe
3–5 large eggs, hard-boiled, in 4–5
segments
Cucumber, fresh, sliced
1–2 tomatoes, in segments
Bunch of dill
Lemon, sliced
Crisp lettuce, ½ head

Directions:

Bread:
Preheat oven to 375°F (190°C). Melt butter and allow it to cool. Line two round 9½" (24 cm) pans, with removable bottoms, with parchment paper. Butter and dust with coconut flour.

In large bowl, beat eggs with a handheld electric mixer until light and airy, approximately three minutes. Add butter and blend well.

In a separate bowl, mix dry ingredients, then blend thoroughly into batter. Let mixture rest at least ten minutes.

Spread mixture evenly in pans and bake in the middle of the oven for about thirty minutes. Cool on a wire rack.

Skagen Filling:
Peel shrimp. If in brine or defrosted, drain properly. Chop shrimp coarsely. In a bowl, mix shrimp with rest of ingredients. Adjust seasoning and add more lemon juice if needed.

Salad Filling:
Mix ingredients in a bowl.

Smoked Salmon Filling:
Chop salmon, hard-boiled eggs, and cress. In a bowl, mix with rest of ingredients. Adjust seasoning and add more lemon juice if needed.

Assembly:
Remove parchment paper and cut each round loaf into two layers.

Place first layer on a serving dish, spread skagen filling, and place next layer on top. Spread salad filling and add next layer. Spread smoked salmon filling and place last layer on top.

Garnish:
Mix mayonnaise, crème fraîche, and some lemon juice, if needed. Cover assembled sandwich with the mixture. Decorate torta by piling shrimp on top and arrange smoked salmon slices around them interspersed with tomato segments and cucumber slices. Cover sides with julienned salad strips and dust the whole loaf with chopped dill.

One-Layer Sandwich Log:
Use bread recipe, but bake in a parchment-lined 6-cup (1419-ml) loaf pan.

Cool completely on a wire rack. Cut off crust along the sides and then cut the loaf lengthwise into four layers.

Slather the layers with fresh butter, layer with crisp lettuce leaves, and line up all your favorite fixings: cheese, ham slices, country pâté, meatballs, salmon, shrimp, tomatoes, and pepper slices. Garnish with olives, dill, lemon, pickled beetroot, and cornichons (or gherkins, depending on preference) and top with a creamy mayonnaise dressing.

Tapas-Style Triangles:
Bake bread in loaf pan. Cool completely on a wire rack. Slice loaf and remove side crusts. Cut slices in half diagonally.

Now butter bread and add your favorite toppings: smoked ham with hot radish dressing, hard-boiled eggs, shrimp and mayonnaise, or anchovies with sour cream.

Index

Acknowledgments

A big thank you to Thomas at Önska and Emma at Iittala Outlet in Borås, Sweden, who kindly provided beautiful tableware for the photographs. The visuals, which are so important to me, take my breath away.

And thank you, Mia, for your invaluable help. You are always so quick to lend me marvelous items and accessories for each photography session.

A huge thank you, Martin! Your beautiful photographs are indispensable for my books, and I and my family have a special place for you in our hearts.

Thank you, Annika, my editor. It has been a great pleasure working with you.

To Lisa, my Swedish publisher, who always listens and understands: you have my warmest hugs and thanks. You're such a fantastic person.

I have to thank my daughter Elisabeth, who always draws great illustrations for my books.

A very special thank you to my mother-in-law Anne-Marie, who is always ready to find the right elements for successful photography sessions.

A huge thank you to my husband Mikael and the rest of my family and friends, who always encourage me, who never hesitate to test my recipes and inventions, and who give me an honest thumbs up or down.

Once again, my heartfelt thank you to all of you!